# I WANT TO BE A
# PILOT

Written & storyboarded by
Jonathan Reule

Illustration
Lina Sanchez

Copyright © 2023 by Unibino Pte. Ltd.





First paperback edition May 2023
ISBN 978-981-18-6522-0

Published by Unibino Pte. Ltd.
31 Rochester Drive Level 3, #03-47 Singapore 138637

www.unibino.com

Pilots help us soar as a society. With hundreds of flights going from country to country every single day, it's quite obvious how important these professionals are to us. But it wasn't always this way. Since the beginning of time, humans have travelled far and wide, and we have pushed ourselves to explore every aspect of our world.

However, travelling on foot could only take us so far. We would watch in envy as birds soar almost weightlessly in the skies above us - flying great distances we could only hope to achieve. It was one place for the longest time that we were unable to travel.

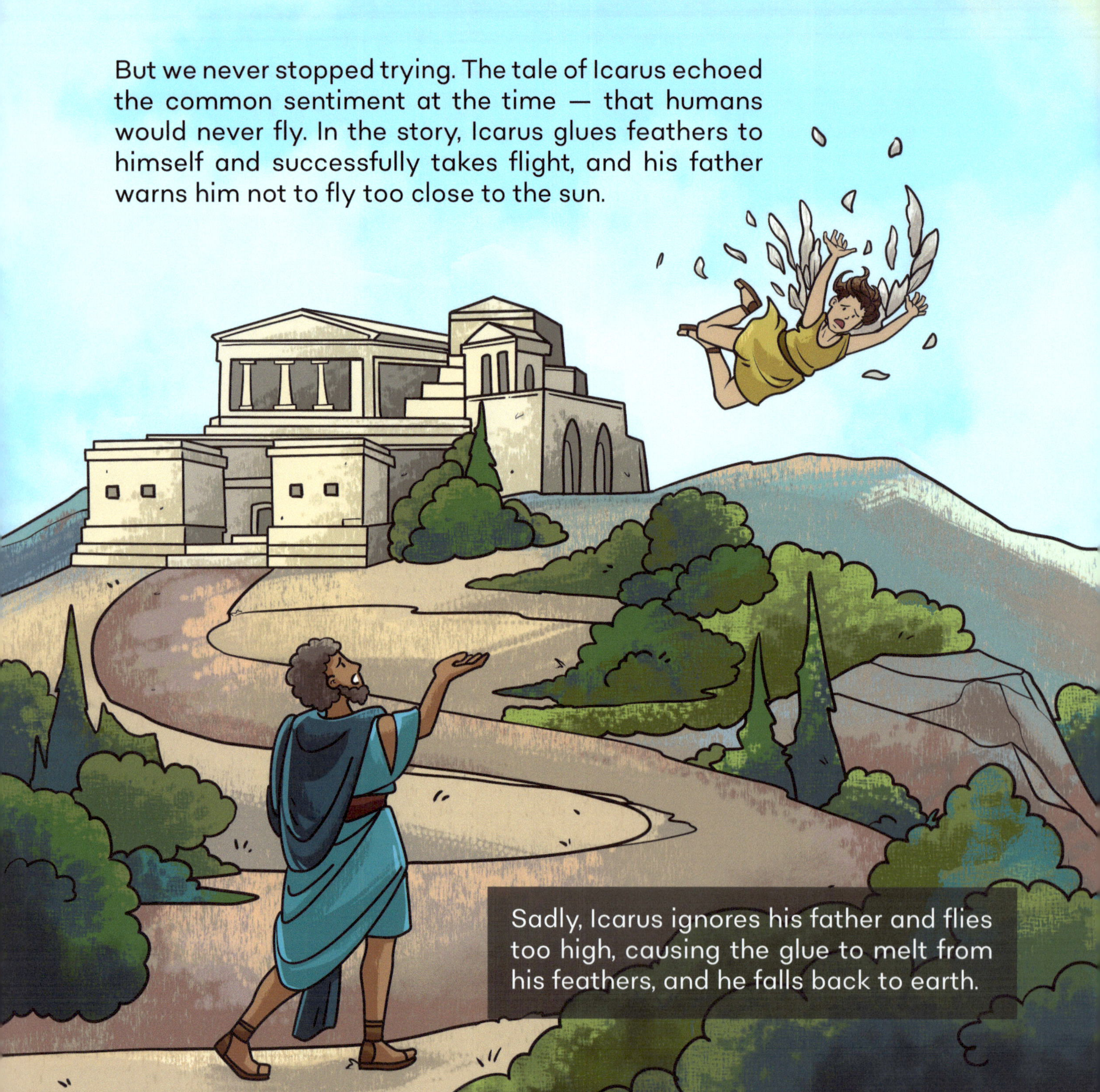

But we never stopped trying. The tale of Icarus echoed the common sentiment at the time — that humans would never fly. In the story, Icarus glues feathers to himself and successfully takes flight, and his father warns him not to fly too close to the sun.

Sadly, Icarus ignores his father and flies too high, causing the glue to melt from his feathers, and he falls back to earth.

Have you heard of the folklore of King Bladud, a king who also pursued the dream of flight? The story goes that he constructed wings onto his back that he professed would allow him to fly.

To prove this, he climbed onto a tall building while the whole town gathered to watch and jumped off the roof, only to fall straight to the ground.

These early blunders were simply stepping stones toward our ultimate goal. No matter how impossible the dream seemed, we still found ways to reach up into the sky, even if we weren't the ones to soar above.

In Ancient China, people expressed their desire for flight by crafting intricate kites, which they would send soaring into the air, controlled by a long string.

These captivating kite displays were very popular, providing a sense of connection between the people and their creations suspended in the sky. In their pursuit of innovation, they even devised man-lifting kites capable of elevating a person, granting them a remarkable experience of soaring through the air.

Through a cycle of failures and improvements, our aspirations of flight gradually transformed into more attainable visions. With the progress of science and technology, we gained deeper insights into the flight patterns of birds, enabling us to make increasingly sophisticated attempts at emulating their aerial prowess.

Leonardo da Vinci, a curious observer of the natural world, delved into the realms of science and mathematics. Armed with his knowledge, he sketched aircraft designs that he believed had the potential to take flight. Upon closer inspection, one can discern an early blueprint that would later serve as inspiration for the development of modern helicopters.

From these more advanced designs came the bravery to test them out. Early attempts involved glider-type contraptions, yet none managed to sustain us in the skies for long durations. It was during this period that we realised the necessity of a substance lighter than air to help us fly. That substance came in the form of hydrogen.

By filling up giant balloons with hydrogen, we discovered that we could lift enough weight from the ground. Finally, we achieved our goal of flight. Soon, we began building more sophisticated machines, such as dirigibles with powerful fans that enabled us to manoeuvre through the skies.

However, we were still not satisfied with our progress. We needed more control over these aircraft and wanted to travel farther and at a faster rate! At the time, steam-powered engines were becoming more popular as they were being used in boats and trains. Eventually, we incorporated such engines into aircraft.

This started the great race to invent an aircraft that could fly, even if it was heavier than air. Several attempts were made, but unfortunately, many of them ended up crashing.

Finally, in 1903, history was made in Kitty Hawk, North Carolina, by the Wright brothers, Wilbur and Orville Wright, when they succeeded in sustaining flight in an aeroplane that was much heavier than air.

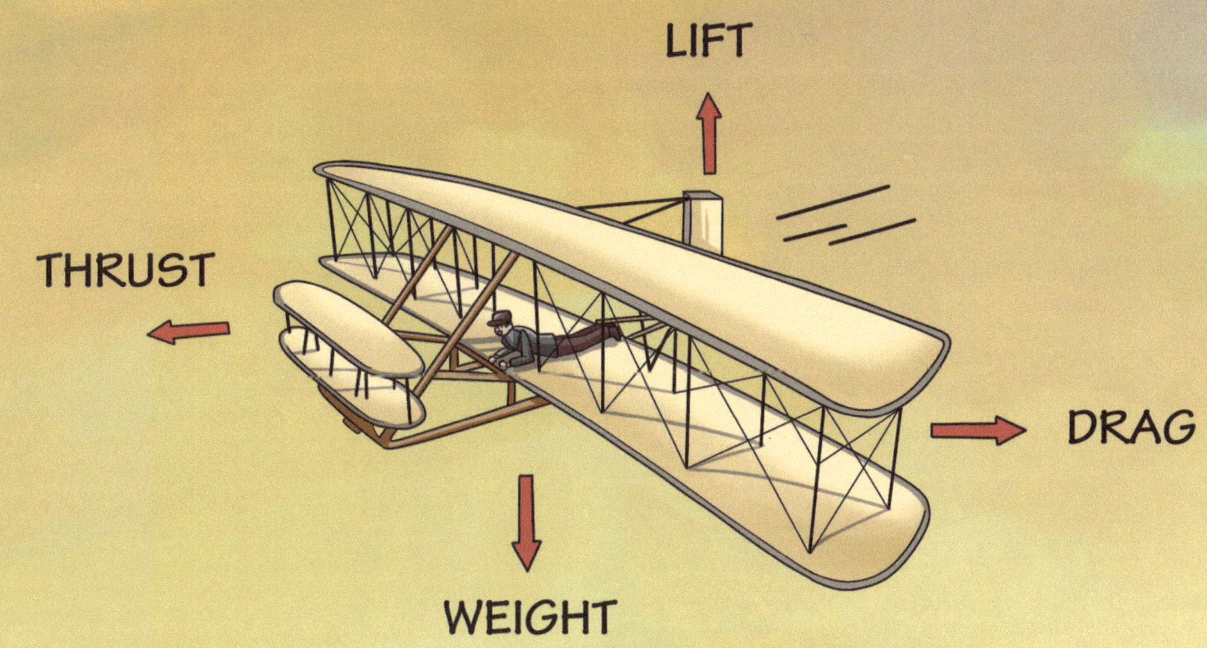

From that day forward, aircraft designs took on a new shape. We learned from the Wright Brothers that in order for these heavy aircraft to rise, we needed four main components: thrust, drag, weight, and lift.

These guiding principles led us to design aircraft that could sustain flight longer and fly faster than ever before. Over the next few decades, more and more aircraft filled the skies. Most of them were made with rotor engines at their noses until the 1940s when German scientists invented the first-ever jet aircraft, which brought us to where we are today in the modern aeronautical world.

In a span of a little over a hundred years, we have made great advances in aeronautical technology. From speedy helicopters that can take you on a wild adventure to soaring commercial jet planes that can send you to another country, we have come a long way from our humble beginnings.

As aircraft become more sophisticated, our need for trained pilots continues to increase. Operating an aeroplane is a distinct skill set, requiring comprehensive training beyond driving a car or piloting a boat. The complexities and considerations involved in flying necessitate rigorous preparation before a pilot can confidently take to the skies solo.

So as you can see, pilots are vitally important in our everyday lives. Even if you don't take a commercial flight or ride around in a helicopter, there are several other ways in which trained pilots benefit our lives. For example, anytime you order an item from overseas, it's likely that those packages are put onto cargo planes for delivery.

If you've ever seen the news about traffic reports or disaster areas that show a bird's eye view, then it's also likely you have a pilot to thank for bringing film crews out in a helicopter to catch those scenes! More importantly, pilots can also play a pivotal role in saving lives. Most of the larger hospitals have their own helicopters that are used in emergency cases to get patients to the hospital faster than any car can manage.

After learning of this information, would you now like to know how to become a pilot? There are several routes you can take. The first step is to know what type of pilot you'd like to be!

Commercial pilots fly big planes with lots of passengers to different places. They can go on journeys from as short as an hour all the way up to eighteen hours at a time! Being a commercial pilot means spending a lot of time in the cockpit and adjusting to different time zones when travelling to other countries.

Aerial firefighting pilots help to stop nasty fires by flying helicopters and planes over infernos and discharging large amounts of water onto the affected areas. Since fires can start at any time of day or night, firefighting pilots must always be ready to receive a call to fly. They have to be brave, too, as they will be flying close to disaster areas.

Search and rescue pilots must be at the ready throughout the day and night as well. They will never know when a call will come in for them to save lives. Search and rescue pilots often fly helicopters, especially above the sea, where boats may capsize, leaving passengers stranded in the water. They can also be called to fly into forests or high up to high mountain tops where hikers have gotten lost or, worse, hurt.

Space pilots are essential for transporting astronauts up into orbit and back down to the Earth. They may also be called upon if there are ever manned missions to the Moon, Mars, or beyond. But for now, they are frequent visitors of the International Space Station, where brilliant scientists from all over the world gather.

Drone pilots are a new branch of aviators. In a world with plenty of flying unmanned machines and robots, these individuals come in handy, with their skills and flying techniques. In fact, it is predicted that this field will only become more developed in time. So it is likely that there will be plenty of job openings for drone operators in the future.

Many different kinds of aircraft require different skills from a pilot. That's why it is important to know what kind of pilot you would like to be so you can tailor your educational journey to fit your aspirations.

No matter what path you choose, there are still basic requirements to fulfil in order to become a pilot. First, it is important to understand how modern airplanes fly. Knowing what makes an aircraft lift from the ground and then soar will help you become a better pilot.

Next, you will need to fulfil a minimum number of supervised flying hours where you practise flying with an experienced instructor. This is where flight schools come in handy as they not only teach you the basics but also offer instructors who will train you to fly.

Alternatively, you can also consider joining the military. You will be trained in the basics like at any other flight institution and paired with an instructor. Most militaries around the world now require their pilots to have at least a bachelor's degree in a science-related field before joining the air force as a pilot.

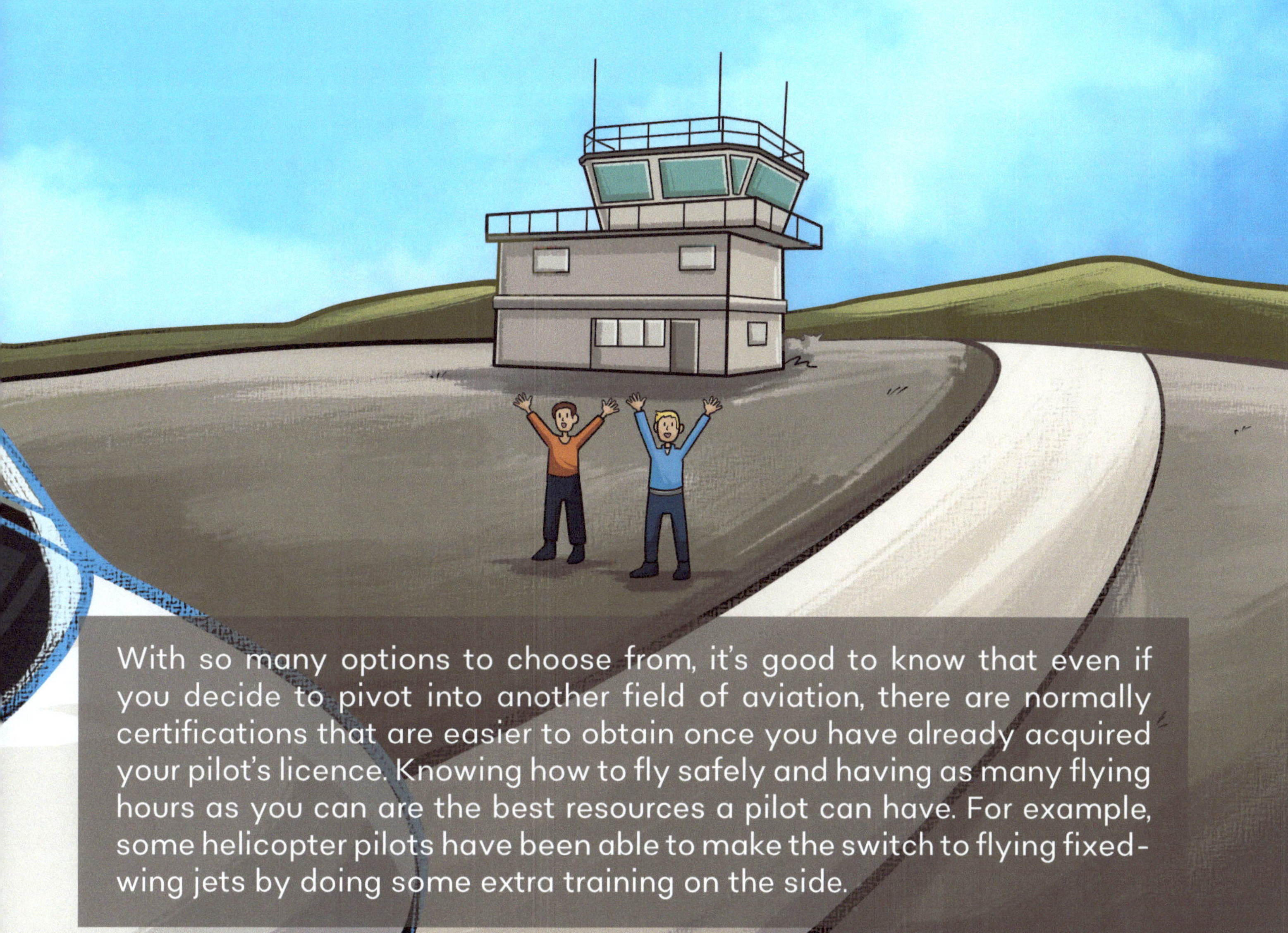

You could also hire a private instructor to train you. This is a great way to become a recreational pilot or even prepare to change careers, as you can book lessons around your schedule. Training with private instructors also means that you receive a more personalised learning experience.

With so many options to choose from, it's good to know that even if you decide to pivot into another field of aviation, there are normally certifications that are easier to obtain once you have already acquired your pilot's licence. Knowing how to fly safely and having as many flying hours as you can are the best resources a pilot can have. For example, some helicopter pilots have been able to make the switch to flying fixed-wing jets by doing some extra training on the side.

But it's up to you to decide if being a pilot fits you best. Should you choose to become a pilot, remember that you can make an impact on many people's lives.

From taking people to different countries and delivering cargo over long distances to transporting emergency patients and saving homes from wildfires, the world is only going to become more reliant on pilots as we go. With this responsibility, it is vital to stay up to date with aviation technology and always give your best on every flight you make.

# My Inspiration

As a parent in this ever-changing world, it can sometimes feel overwhelming when it comes to our children's futures. New technologies seem to be arising almost every day, and with so many innovations, it creates unique professions which many of us wouldn't have dreamed to be necessary only a few years ago. Which to me is a good thing. Because with so much variety, my children can have the opportunity to pick a career that will fit their personalities and build upon their strengths. As you may imagine, this desire within me to provide my children with the resources they needed to thrive, led me to search out books that would be easy enough for them to understand while teaching them about various professions.

**Shubhi Saxena**
**Founder, Unibino**

Only, I found that these books were few and far between. Even if I could find a book about a certain profession geared towards young readers, I found them sparse inside and limited to only certain careers that may not fit my children's abilities. This is when I came up with the idea to write my own children's books, teaching them about all the various careers in the modern world. After months of researching different professions and learning more than I ever expected, I quickly realised this was going to be a bigger project than I first anticipated. I dove into the histories of these professions, discovering links to the past, and why these professions were now so important.

Ultimately my goal was to offer my children options, to show them that there is no one set path for everyone. But in this, I stumbled upon something bigger. I wanted to share this with future generations. To share with all children and parents about these careers, to help spark curiosity, and to instil a passion for the future. Everyone has special talents and abilities, and I hope that this series will be able to offer clarity and inspiration to children around the world. Because at the end of the day, it's never too early to start dreaming and never too late to take action. With this, I hope you enjoy this series and that your young ones become the best versions of themselves as they can achieve.